Intermediate 2

English

2004 Exam
Close Reading
Critical Essay

2005 Exam
Close Reading
Critical Essay

2006 Exam
Close Reading
Critical Essay

2007 Exam
Close Reading
Critical Essay

2008 Exam
Close Reading
Critical Essay

Leckie ✕ Leckie

First exam published in 2004.
Published by Leckie & Leckie Ltd, 3rd Floor, 4 Queen Street, Edinburgh EH2 1JE
tel: 0131 220 6831 fax: 0131 225 9987 enquiries@leckieandleckie.co.uk www.leckieandleckie.co.uk

ISBN 978-1-84372-659-3

A CIP Catalogue record for this book is available from the British Library.

Leckie & Leckie is a division of Huveaux plc.

Leckie & Leckie is grateful to the copyright holders, as credited at the back of the book, for permission to use their material.
Every effort has been made to trace the copyright holders and to obtain their permission for the use of copyright material.
Leckie & Leckie will gladly receive information enabling them to rectify any error or omission in subsequent editions.

[BLANK PAGE]

X115/201

NATIONAL
QUALIFICATIONS
2004

FRIDAY, 14 MAY
1.00 PM – 2.00 PM

ENGLISH
INTERMEDIATE 2
Close Reading

Answer all questions.

30 marks are allocated to this paper.

Read the passage carefully and then answer **all** the questions, **using your own words as far as possible**.

The questions will ask you to show that:

> you understand the main ideas and important details in the passage—in other words, **what** the writer has said (**Understanding—U**);

> you can identify, using appropriate terms, the techniques the writer has used to get across these ideas—in other words, **how** he has said it (**Analysis—A**);

> you can, using appropriate evidence, comment on how effective the writer has been—in other words, **how well** he has said it (**Evaluation—E**).

A code letter (U, A, E) is used alongside each question to identify its purpose for you. The number of marks attached to each question will give some indication of the length of answer required.

The passage which follows is adapted from an article in the Travel section of a newspaper. In it, Sean Newsom tells of his experience as a trainee guide in the African bush.

Playing at Guide and Seek

At some point in their lives, everybody has been at this place. Maybe they were waiting to give a best man's speech with not one good joke in it. Or perhaps it was outside a school hall before the start of an exam. And I'm pretty sure they all felt the same thing: as if they had just jumped out of a plane at the start of their first-ever sky dive, and
5 realised they had forgotten their parachute.

In 45 minutes I will lead a walking safari through the African bush – with only five days' training under my belt. That's right, dear reader: six days ago I knew as much about the fauna and flora of East Africa as I did about the contents of your fridge. Now I am going to lead six strangers into a two-mile stretch of savannah and attempt to turn this brown
10 world of dry vegetation and nervous, secretive animals into a colourful and exciting abundance of biological complexity. And I'm going to attempt to do so without anyone getting hurt.

Actually, there's very little chance that we are going to meet anything dangerous. This is the Saadani, not the Serengeti. It's a small game reserve on the coast, north of Dar-es-
15 Salaam, and although there are plenty of animals here – from a kaleidoscope of kingfishers to a wide range of buck, giraffes and even lions – it's also the site of one of the oldest settlements in Tanzania. The presence of humans long ago taught the local carnivore populations who really is the king of the jungle. Just in case one of them attempts a takeover, however, we're going to be accompanied by an armed warden. Dave
20 will be there too.

That's not what I'm worried about. What really concerns me is the fact that, in order to make this test a little more "interesting" as he puts it, Dave has decided not to tell his clients who I am. Bit of a surprise, that. After all, this course is not supposed to be the real thing. It's more of a taster, at least, that's what I thought. Now, however, I am faced
25 by the prospect of six trusting souls who all think I'm an expert. And I am terrifyingly short of the information that I need. Don't get me wrong, Dave has done his best to prepare me for this moment. Working with a specially prepared training manual, he's introduced me to the vast range of skills that a safari guide needs. We've worked on Jeep and boat handling, plant and animal identification, tracking, safety, conservation issues
30 and local politics. We've travelled from Dar-es-Salaam to the magnificent and undeveloped Selous Game Reserve, and then to a beachfront camp in the Saadani. And all the time, Dave has been talking.

That's the problem, really. Every time he opens his mouth there is something new to remember. It might be a little titbit of information that is going to liven up a dull
35 moment out in the bush, such as the recent discovery of a whole system of low-frequency murmurings that elephants use to keep in contact with each other. There's so much fascinating stuff to learn about this place, and that's before you've got to the tricky business of remembering what everything is called. One by one, Dave throws names at me. One by one, I forget them.

40 You can imagine what the walking safari is like. There is a brief moment of triumph at the start when I manage to get an antlion to perform for us. Antlions are little grubs that live in the ground and excavate cone-shaped holes in the soil. They're expert hunters and perfect examples of how murderous the bush is, even when the animals

involved are smaller than your fingernail. They also happen to be a useful way of
45 keeping your clients entertained when there is nothing more glamorous to look at. The reason why antlions dig their holes is because they want ants to fall into them and provide them with a meal, and – lo! – just as I'm telling my group this, along comes an ant and tumbles into the miniature death-pit. He's too big for this particular grub, however, and after a struggle, he escapes. But he's proved my point perfectly. My clients
50 are excited. So am I.

From then on, however, a more familiar pattern reasserts itself. My warden leads us into a thicket of whistling thorn acacia that seems to be half a mile thick. I dutifully say my piece on whistling thorn acacia. After a minute or two, I start to get nervous. After five, I am beginning to panic.

55 So it's with a huge wash of relief that eventually I spot a medium-sized, brilliantly-coloured bird, flitting between the trees. "Hey, everyone!" I call. "It's a lilac-backed roller!" And I take a look through my binoculars. That's when I realise that actually it doesn't have a lilac-coloured back at all. Its breast is lilac. It's a lilac-breasted roller, one of the most common birds on the savannah. The kind you never, ever, misidentify. It's as
60 if I've just called a blackbird a robin.

It gets worse. Because when I turn back to see if anybody has noticed, I realise that they're all looking the other way. The reason? Well, it turns out that we are no more than 50 yards from a small herd of giraffe. Actually, it's 100 yards now. Not only was I the last to spot them, my shouting has scared them off.

65 By the time we reach the salt flats that mark the end of our route, I am ready to leave everybody behind and carry on walking into the sea. The sun is beginning to set now, and there is just enough time to check out the latest animal prints in the sand before we climb into the waiting Land Rover for the drive home. I sit down next to the driver and my whole body goes slack with relief.

70 All that lies ahead of me is one last hurdle of embarrassment, when we tell the clients who I am. Then we'll all go down to the beach, light a big bonfire and drink a lot of beer. Occasionally, I'll let my head drop back and look up, through the clear Tanzanian air, at the brilliant night sky. I'll reflect on what an extraordinary week it's been. And I'll ask the stars to grant me one small request.

75 Can I do that again?

Adapted from an article in *The Sunday Times*

QUESTIONS   *Marks Code*

1. Explain how the context of the first paragraph helps you to understand what the writer means by ". . . everybody has been at this place." (line 1).   2   U

2. Look again at lines 6–12.

   (a) How does the punctuation help to convey how worried and unprepared the writer feels?   1   A

   (b) How does the writer establish a conversational tone?   1   A

   (c) How does the writer's contrasting word choice in the sentence beginning "Now I am going to lead . . ." (lines 8–9) convey the difficulty of his task?   2   A

3. Show how the sentence "That's not what I'm worried about." (line 21) is a successful link between paragraphs 3 and 4.   2   A

4. Look again at lines 21–32.

   What are the writer's two main concerns?   2   U

5. Comment on the effectiveness of the structure of the final two sentences in lines 38–39.   2   A

6. In what **two** ways did the writer think the antlion's performance provided him with ". . . a brief moment of triumph . . ." (line 40)?   2   U

7. "From then on, however, a more familiar pattern reasserts itself." (line 51)

   Why does the writer describe the pattern in this way?   2   U

8. Which expression from lines 51–54 shows that the writer lacks enthusiasm for this part of his task?   1   U

9. (a) Look again at lines 55–60.

      Identify by example any **two techniques** the writer uses to convey his stupidity, and comment on their effectiveness.   4   E

   (b) Why does the writer feel a "huge wash of relief" when he sees a "brilliantly-coloured bird" (lines 55–56)?   1   U

10. Explain clearly why the writer feels "It gets worse." (line 61).   2   U

11. What image does the writer use in the second last paragraph (lines 70–74) to show that he felt the safari had been an ordeal, and how does it do so?   2   A

12. Explain how the short final paragraph (line 75) achieves its impact.   2   A

13. In what ways might "Playing at Guide and Seek" be considered a particularly appropriate title for this article?   2   E

Total (30)

[END OF QUESTION PAPER]

X115/202

NATIONAL
QUALIFICATIONS
2004

FRIDAY, 14 MAY
2.20 PM – 3.50 PM

ENGLISH
INTERMEDIATE 2
Critical Essay

Answer **two** questions.

Each question must be taken from a different section.

Each question is worth 25 marks.

SCOTTISH
QUALIFICATIONS
AUTHORITY

©

Answer TWO questions from this paper.

Each question must be chosen from a different Section (A–E). You are not allowed to choose two questions from the same Section.

In all Sections you may use Scottish texts.

Write the number of each question in the margin of your answer booklet and begin each essay on a fresh page. You should spend about 45 minutes on each essay.

The following will be assessed:

- **the relevance of your essays to the questions you have chosen**

- **the quality of your writing**

- **the technical accuracy of your writing.**

Each answer is worth up to 25 marks. The total for this paper is 50 marks.

SECTION A—DRAMA

1. Choose a play in which one of the main characters has to overcome difficulties in the course of the action.

   State what the difficulties are and show how the character's strengths allow him or her to overcome them.

   In your answer you must refer to the text and to at least **two** of: characterisation, plot, key scenes, theme, or any other appropriate feature.

2. Choose a play in which there is conflict between two important characters.

   Show how the conflict arises and go on to explain how, by the end of the play, it is or is not resolved.

   In your answer you must refer to the text and to at least **two** of: characterisation, dialogue, key scenes, structure, or any other appropriate feature.

3. Choose a play with a violent theme.

   State what the theme is and show how the characters deal with the issues in such a way as either to overcome the violence or to be destroyed by it.

   In your answer you must refer to the text and to at least **two** of: theme, characterisation, climax, key scenes, or any other appropriate feature.

SECTION B—PROSE

4. Choose a novel or short story which deals with family life.

    Show how the relationships within the family affect the events and outcome of the story.

    In your answer you must refer to the text and to at least **two** of: plot, key scenes, characterisation, or any other appropriate feature.

5. Choose a novel or a short story which has an unexpected ending.

    By looking at the story as a whole explain why the ending is surprising, and explain whether you found it satisfactory or not.

    In your answer you must refer to the text and to at least **two** of: structure, characterisation, plot, climax, or any other appropriate feature.

6. Choose a prose work or group of prose works (fiction or non-fiction) dealing to some extent with a less pleasant side of life.

    Show how this less pleasant side of life is portrayed and made more real for you by the description of the people and/or places and/or events.

    In your answer you must refer to the text, and to at least **two** of: theme, language, structure, setting, or any other appropriate feature.

SECTION C—POETRY

7. Choose a poem which deals with a real or imaginary person or place.

    Show how the person or place is introduced and how the techniques used give a convincing portrayal of that person or place.

    In your answer you must refer to the text and to at least **two** of: characterisation, imagery, word choice, tone, or any other appropriate feature.

8. Choose a poem which takes an optimistic view of life.

    Briefly state what the poem is about and go on to show how the techniques used convey these optimistic feelings.

    In your answer you must refer to the text and to at least **two** of: theme, imagery, word choice, structure, or any other appropriate feature.

9. Choose a poem which tells an exciting or frightening story.

    Briefly state what the story is and go on to show how the techniques used make the poem exciting or frightening.

    In your answer you must refer to the text and to at least **two** of: tone, word choice, imagery, rhythm, or any other appropriate feature.

[Turn over

SECTION D—MASS MEDIA

10. Choose a film or *TV drama which has war as its subject.

    Show how the film, by its use of content and techniques, has brought home to you the reality of the terrible nature of war.

    In your answer you must refer to the text and to at least **two** of: theme, editing, use of camera, music, or any other appropriate feature.

11. Choose a film or *TV drama which deals with conflict within the family.

    Show what conflict within the family is portrayed and show what media techniques are used to make the conflict dramatic.

    In your answer you must refer to the text and to at least **two** of: characterisation, editing, use of camera, mise-en-scène, or any other appropriate feature.

12. Choose a film or *TV drama which deals with the subject of "good versus evil".

    Briefly explain the struggle and show how your sympathy was engaged on one side or the other.

    In your answer you must refer to the text and to at least **two** of: characterisation, editing, mise-en-scène, or any other appropriate feature.

    * "TV drama" may be a single play, series or serial.

SECTION E—LANGUAGE

13. Consider examples of language used by at least **two** different newspapers or magazines.

    Describe the differences which you have noticed and discuss what you think causes these differences.

    You must refer to specific examples, and to at least **two** of: register, typography, point of view, or any other appropriate feature.

14. Consider the spoken language of a particular place, for example a town, a city, an area, a country.

    What are some of the main features which are important in making this language a distinctive way of speaking? What are the advantages or disadvantages for people speaking this distinctive language?

    You must refer to specific examples, and to at least **two** of: dialect, vocabulary, accent, or any other appropriate feature.

15. Consider language used in campaigns designed to influence people's behaviour in a particular area of their lives, for example to improve their health, to support a charity or other organisation, to buy certain products.

    Explain how the language is designed to influence people, and whether you think it succeeds in affecting their behaviour.

    You must refer to specific examples and to at least **two** of: tone, emotive vocabulary, slogans, or any other appropriate feature.

[END OF QUESTION PAPER]

[BLANK PAGE]

X115/201

NATIONAL	FRIDAY, 13 MAY	ENGLISH
QUALIFICATIONS	1.00 PM – 2.00 PM	INTERMEDIATE 2
2005		Close Reading

Answer all questions.

30 marks are allocated to this paper.

Read the passage carefully and then answer **all** the questions, **using your own words as far as possible**.

The questions will ask you to show that:

> you understand the main ideas and important details in the passage—in other words, **what** the writer has said (**Understanding—U**);

> you can identify, using appropriate terms, the techniques the writer has used to get across these ideas—in other words, **how** he has said it (**Analysis—A**);

> you can, using appropriate evidence, comment on how effective the writer has been—in other words, **how well** he has said it (**Evaluation—E**).

A code letter (U, A, E) is used alongside each question to identify its purpose for you. The number of marks attached to each question will give some indication of the length of answer required.

In this extract from the opening chapter of his book, Ralph Storer reflects upon his need to climb mountains.

Why?

It occurs to all of us at one time or another. Perhaps we are gasping for air on some interminable mountain slope that seems to get steeper at every step without bringing us any closer to the elusive summit. Perhaps we are trembling on some disintegrating rock ledge from where all routes onward seem to involve moves at which Spiderman would
5 baulk. Perhaps we are huddled behind a scrap of cairn on some windswept ridge while the blizzard howls around us. Perhaps we are standing knee-deep in a morass of sodden peat that we were confident would hold our weight. It is in situations like this that it hits us: why am I doing this?

From whence comes this compulsion to climb mountains? My neighbours seem to be
10 able to enjoy lives of quiet contentment without ever having to leave the horizontal plane. Why do I have this compulsion to get to the top of every insignificant bump on the landscape? I ponder this question not in the hope of providing an explanation for my neighbours, still less in the hope of converting them, but out of a need to explain this outlandish behaviour to myself. If I am to climb mountains I would simply like to know
15 why. Why, no matter how breathless, bruised, battered and bedraggled I become while hillwalking, do I return with a grin on my face and a desire to go out and do it again?

The first thought that occurs to me is not *why* but *why not*? Our close relatives the apes enjoy climbing, so why not us? Perhaps the desire to get to the top of things is an ancient animal drive that modern society has suppressed. After all, a society geared to
20 material gain can hardly be expected to support such an unproductive pursuit (the only material gain I've made on the hill is finding a glove that didn't fit). Then again, perhaps the act of climbing is simply too ape-like and unsophisticated for most; it is difficult, for example, to maintain any semblance of dignity while lying spread-eagled on the ground after having tripped over a clump of heather. Ironically, the freedom to
25 adopt such a position and have no-one give disapproving looks is one of the secret joys of hillwalking . . . The Great Outdoors is a giant funhouse where we can cast off adult worries and become carefree kids again. It's no accident that children love climbing.

Yet there must be more to it than a desire to have fun, or else why do I keep going when it ceases to be fun? When I'm cold and tired and out of breath, why do I keep putting
30 one foot in front of the other and, when I've returned to the comfort of my home, why do I recall these times with a glow of satisfaction? Perhaps it has something to do with exercise and fitness — the feelgood feeling that comes from muscles that don't ache when you climb stairs, lungs that don't wheeze when you run for a bus and endorphins that buzz round your head and keep you feeling high even after you have returned to
35 sea-level.

I have heard those whose brains have become as useless as their legs equate hillwalking to banging your head against a brick wall, reasoning that you feel good afterwards simply because you have stopped. Such people, perhaps equating effort with pain in order to justify their own laziness, do not appear to be able to appreciate that effort can be
40 rewarding. Moreover, there are some hillwalkers who seem to find the activity hardly any effort at all. I have a friend who is "naturally" fit, whatever that means. He smokes, drinks and leads a generally debauched life, but stand him at the foot of a hill, let go of him and he will leave even Naismith trailing in his wake.

Bill Naismith, the "father" of the Scottish Mountaineering Club, is a hard man to keep
45 up with at the best of times, even though the ground hasn't seen the imprint of his boots
for some time now. If you can keep to his pace of three miles per hour plus one thousand
feet per half hour (metricated to five kilometres per hour plus one hundred metres per
ten minutes), count yourself fit. On British hills that is normally a pace most walkers
can only attain in dreams.

50 But why do I exert myself on the hill rather than on an athletics track or a tennis court?
And why do I find myself exploring the limits of my fitness? Sometimes, after reaching
the first summit, I go on to a second. In my more bewildered moments, with my eyes on
the ground and my feet firmly in the clouds, I have even been known to climb two
separate mountains on the same day. Now that's serious.

55 Perhaps it has something to do with the challenge. I am sometimes amazed by what I
will attempt on the hill, but I am also amazed by what I learn about myself by doing so
and perhaps this is why I do it. On the other hand, cycling around city streets is just as
risky and physically challenging, so there has to be something still more to it. Perhaps it
has something to do with the environment in which hillwalking takes place — outside,
60 away from city streets, in air that has not been breathed by others.

In Victorian times people took to the seaside to escape the dark satanic mills; now it is
the countryside that beckons. They say it began in the depressed thirties, when
northerners escaped to the Lake District, midlanders to North Wales and lowland Scots
to the Highlands. I know the pull, having myself been job-bound in the Big Smoke and
65 desperate to get away. Some citydwellers become so conditioned to city life that they
cannot live without the noise and bustle of traffic and a regular intake of carbon
monoxide; they may well prove to be a mutant species, an evolutionary dead-end
divorced from the mainstream of life. If pushed I will grudgingly admit to an
understanding of the excitements of city life, but I also need my Arcadian fix. I need
70 terrain other than concrete, greenery other than lawns, an horizon more distant than the
end of the street, weather I cannot shelter from and smells from which I am not
insulated. Without these I wither away like a plant without light.

Adapted from *The Joy of Hillwalking* by Ralph Storer

QUESTIONS

Marks Code

1. Look at lines 1–8.

    (*a*) Quote **two** expressions which make hillwalking sound a rather unpleasant and uncomfortable activity.

    2 A

    (*b*) Quote the **word** which the writer uses to suggest that sometimes the summit seems beyond reach.

    1 A

2. "It occurs to all of us at one time or another." (line 1)

    From your reading of the whole paragraph explain what "It" is.

    1 A

3. In lines 9–16, the writer reflects on his need to climb mountains.

    By referring to **one** example of each, show how he demonstrates this need through:

    (*a*) word choice;

    2 A

    (*b*) sentence structure.

    2 A

4. Read lines 17–27 again.

    In your own words, give the **two** reasons the writer uses to explain people's desire to climb hills. Quote briefly to support each reason.

    4 U

5. Explain how the sentence "Yet there must be more to . . . it ceases to be fun?" (lines 28–29) performs a linking function.

    2 A

6. Using your own words as far as possible, summarise the **three** reasons the writer gives in lines 31–35 for returning to the hills despite all the obvious discomforts.

    3 U

7. Look at lines 36–40.

    What is the writer's attitude towards those who do not appreciate hillwalking? Justify your answer by **two** close references to the text.

    3 U/A

8. What is suggested by the comment about Naismith that "the ground hasn't seen the imprint of his boots for some time now"? (lines 45–46)

    1 U

9. In lines 55–60, the writer begins two sentences with "Perhaps".

    (*a*) How does this word link with the previous paragraph (lines 50–54)?

    1 A

    (*b*) What effect does it have on the tone of this paragraph (lines 55–60)?

    1 A

10. Look again at the sentence "In Victorian times people took to the seaside to escape the dark satanic mills; now it is the countryside that beckons." (lines 61–62)

     Identify and give an example of **one** technique the writer uses to achieve the effect of balance or contrast.

     2 A

11. In the final paragraph (lines 61–72), the writer describes how it is not new for people to be "desperate to get away". With reference to **one** example explain fully, in your own words, how he illustrates this point.

     2 U

12. "Without these I wither away like a plant without light." (line 72)

     Comment on the effectiveness of this sentence as a conclusion to the whole passage.

     3 E

[END OF QUESTION PAPER]

Total (30)

X115/202

NATIONAL
QUALIFICATIONS
2005

FRIDAY, 13 MAY
2.20 PM – 3.50 PM

ENGLISH
INTERMEDIATE 2
Critical Essay

Answer **two** questions.

Each question must be taken from a different section.

Each question is worth 25 marks.

SCOTTISH
QUALIFICATIONS
AUTHORITY
©

Answer **TWO** questions from this paper.

Each question must be chosen from a different Section (A–E). You are not allowed to choose two questions from the same Section.

In all Sections you may use Scottish texts.

Write the number of each question in the margin of your answer booklet and begin each essay on a fresh page. You should spend about 45 minutes on each essay.

The following will be assessed:

- the relevance of your essays to the questions you have chosen

- the quality of your writing

- the technical accuracy of your writing.

Each answer is worth up to 25 marks. The total for this paper is 50 marks.

SECTION A—DRAMA

1. Choose a play in which **one** of the main characters has to cope with strong feelings such as love, jealousy, ambition, hatred.

   Show how the character deals with these feelings and what effect this has on the outcome of the play.

   In your answer you must refer to the text and at least **two** of: characterisation, theme, structure, or any other appropriate feature.

2. Choose a scene from a play in which a conflict between two characters reaches a climax.

   Explain the origins of the conflict and show how the outcome of the scene influences the rest of the play.

   In your answer you must refer to the text and to at least **two** of: structure, characterisation, plot, or any other appropriate feature.

3. Choose a play which explores relationships within a family or community.

   What strengths and/or weaknesses are apparent in these relationships and what is the overall effect on the family or community?

   In your answer you must refer to the text and to at least **two** of: characterisation, theme, structure, or any other appropriate feature.

SECTION B—PROSE

4. Choose a novel or short story in which a character changes in the course of the story.

   What factors seem to cause the development? What effect does this have on the character and on the outcome of the story?

   In your answer you must refer to the text and to at least **two** of: characterisation, plot, key incident, or any other appropriate feature.

5. Choose a prose work or a group of prose works (fiction or non-fiction) which deals with a topic of interest to you.

   Explain how your interest was aroused and how the treatment of the theme or topic contributed to your enjoyment of the work.

   In your answer you must refer to the text and to at least **two** of: theme, ideas, description, structure, or any other appropriate feature.

6. Choose a novel or short story in which you feel there is an incident of great importance.

   Briefly describe the incident and go on to highlight its importance in the story as a whole.

   In your answer you must refer to the text and to at least **two** of: structure, characterisation, plot, climax, or any other appropriate feature.

SECTION C—POETRY

7. Choose a poem which creates a mood of calm, or reflection, or nostalgia.

   Show how the poet creates this mood by the choice of subject matter and by the use of particular poetic techniques.

   In your answer you must refer to the text and to at least **two** of: content, word choice, tone, sound, or any other appropriate feature.

8. Choose a poem which describes a positive experience.

   Describe what happens in the poem, and show how the poet, by the use of poetic techniques, has enhanced your appreciation of the positive aspects of the poem.

   In your answer you must refer to the text and to at least **two** of: word choice, tone, imagery, sound, or any other appropriate feature.

9. Choose a poem which deepens your understanding of human nature.

   State what particular aspect of human nature is explored and show how the poet's choice of content and use of poetic techniques deepens your understanding.

   In your answer you must refer to the text and to at least **two** of: content, word choice, theme, imagery, or any other appropriate feature.

[Turn over

SECTION D—MASS MEDIA

10. Choose a film in which there is a sequence of great importance to the development of character and/or plot.

    Show how elements of character and/or plot are developed in this sequence to create impact.

    In your answer you must refer to the text and to at least **two** of: use of camera, characterisation, editing, sound effects, or any other appropriate feature.

11. Choose a film or TV drama* in which the portrayal of the setting is very important to the success of the film or TV drama.

    Show how the setting is used to increase your appreciation of character and theme in the film or TV drama.

    In your answer you must refer to the text and to at least **two** of: mise-en-scène, use of camera, editing, or any other appropriate feature.

12. Choose a film or TV drama* which seems to reflect contemporary society.

    How successful do you feel the film or TV drama is in convincing the audience that it is giving a true reflection of society today?

    In your answer you must refer to the text and to at least **two** of: theme, setting, dialogue, characterisation, or any other appropriate feature.

    * "TV drama" may be a single play, series or serial.

SECTION E—LANGUAGE

13. Consider your own use of spoken language in different situations.

    Give examples of what the different situations are and go on to discuss how these different situations affect your use of spoken language.

    In your answer you must refer to specific examples and to at least **two** concepts such as context, register, dialect, accent, or any other appropriate feature.

14. Consider the language of advertisements.

    By looking closely at the language of TWO advertisements, state which one you think is more effective in persuading you to buy the product.

    In your answer you must refer to specific examples and to at least **two** concepts such as tone, typography, emotive vocabulary, or any other appropriate feature.

15. Consider aspects of vocabulary connected with the use of the Internet.

    Examine some of the words associated with the use of the Internet and consider how helpful this language is for the general user.

    In your answer you must refer to specific examples and to at least **two** concepts such as jargon, abbreviations, imagery, or any other appropriate feature.

[END OF QUESTION PAPER]

X115/201

NATIONAL QUALIFICATIONS 2006	FRIDAY, 12 MAY 1.00 PM – 2.00 PM	ENGLISH INTERMEDIATE 2 Close Reading

Answer all questions.

30 marks are allocated to this paper.

Read the passage carefully and then answer **all** the questions, **using your own words as far as possible**.

The questions will ask you to show that:

> you understand the main ideas and important details in the passage—in other words, **what** the writer has said (**Understanding—U**);

> you can identify, using appropriate terms, the techniques the writer has used to get across these ideas—in other words, **how** he has said it (**Analysis—A**);

> you can, using appropriate evidence, comment on how effective the writer has been—in other words, **how well** he has said it (**Evaluation—E**).

A code letter (U, A, E) is used alongside each question to identify its purpose for you. The number of marks attached to each question will give some indication of the length of answer required.

SCOTTISH QUALIFICATIONS AUTHORITY

Women and chocolate: Simply made for each other

Women and chocolate are a dream team and advertisers have cleverly ensured they stay that way.

You can bet that when the first Aztec tentatively crushed a cacao bean, right behind him was an ad executive excitedly branding the muddy brown discovery "the food of the gods". Or if there wasn't, there certainly should have been—because chocolate hasn't looked back since. Mars' new "Mars Delight" is just the latest attempt to beguile us into
5 seeing that a mixture of fat, sugar and a type of caffeine is an essential part of our life.

The secret of chocolate's particular appeal lies in the cocoa butter—it melts just below body temperature—which gives it that delicious dissolve-in-the-mouth feeling. Add to that the sudden charge of energy you get from the sugar, the kick of the caffeine and another chemical, which acts as a mood enhancer—and you can understand why the
10 Aztecs originally decreed that only nobles, priests and warriors were allowed to eat it. Then it was seen as the cure for all ills. And it's true—as the confectionery industry is keen to point out—that cocoa beans contain flavonoids which help high blood pressure. And chocolate doesn't have the teeth-rotting qualities of other sweets.

But that's more than counterbalanced by the fact that it's still crammed full of fats and
15 sugar. "We are looking at 9 to 10 calories per gram," says Professor Tom Sanders, the head of nutritional sciences at King's College, London. "And while people admit to eating 18 grams of chocolate a day, the manufacturers think it's nearer 35 grams, about the size of a Crunchie bar. What's also worrying is the trend to "super-size" that we also see in the fast food industry that means that people end up consuming more. Of
20 particular concern is that chocolate bars contain vegetable fats—also known as trans fatty acids (TFAs)—which have been linked to coronary heart disease." Last summer both Nestlé and Cadbury said they were thinking of removing TFAs from their products.

"The Government recommends that less than 2 per cent of dietary energy comes from trans fats," says Hannah Theobald, nutrition scientist at the British Nutrition
25 Foundation. "It is good news that the food industry is looking at ways to reduce them in food products."

Ironically, these concerns are far removed from chocolate's beginnings—when, being made by teetotal Quakers, it was originally promoted here as a healthy alternative to alcohol. One of the first recorded advertisements was a couple of lines in the
30 Birmingham Gazette of March 1, 1824, placed by a John Cadbury. It read: "John Cadbury is desirous of introducing to particular notice 'Cocoa Nibs' prepared by himself, an article affording a most nutritious beverage for breakfast".

The nutritious link was one that early chocolate marketing followed. During the Second World War, manufacturers Caley's urged that female air raid wardens should be bought
35 a box of their Fortune chocolates not just because they'd enjoy them but because it would supply the "extra nutrition to keep them going". Early Mars advertising informed women that there was a "whole meal" in a bar to "nourish, energise and sustain".

"Women are the key to chocolate advertising," says Rita Clifton, the chair of the leading
40 branding agency Interbrand. "They are not only important consumers in their own right but they also act as gatekeepers to the rest of the family. So it's important to get the approach right." So as women's role in society changed so did the chocolate bars and advertising. Out went the stoic "meal on the run" idea, in came the post-Sixties "Me" sense of indulgence—running through fields or sitting in a bath eating a flaky chocolate
45 bar. "One of the most 'indulgent' adverts is the Flake one," Clifton says. "This is the

ultimate example of taking time out for yourself. OK, I could never quite see the point of eating a Flake in the bath—not very practical, but then fantasies aren't meant to be."

But experts say that in recent years the style has changed again. The Milk Tray man was kicked out in favour of the slogan "love with a lighter touch". The fashion,
50 according to Yusuf Chuku, a communications analyst at Naked Communications, is very much towards a lighter, more sophisticated approach. "Because of concerns about advertising to children, I think there's been even more of a move towards targeting women," Chuku says. "With health advice constantly changing, I think advertising is now less about the guilty secret idea, but saying it's OK to eat some chocolate as long as
55 you balance it with other things."

That's reflected in the different types of chocolate being developed—low calorie bars like Flyte, "lighter" bars than the monolithic-looking Mars or Snickers, or developments like Kit Kat Kubes, which can be shared among friends. It also explains the increased demand for organic or more exotic chocolates: if women are going to indulge, they want
60 to make sure it is with a high quality brand. Chuku says that in a competitive market worth £5 billion a year in the UK, no manufacturer can afford to miss which way the wind is blowing: "I think the next trend will be turning back to comforting chocolates you remember from your childhood. Watch out for the Wagon Wheel."

Glenda Cooper, in *The Times Body and Soul* (slightly adapted)

QUESTIONS

Marks Code

1. Explain what is meant by the idea that chocolate "hasn't looked back" (lines 3–4) since it was discovered.

   1 U/A

2. Identify and briefly explain any example of humour from the first paragraph.

   2 A

3. Explain **in your own words** two of the reasons why chocolate has its "particular appeal". (line 6)

   2 U

4. Explain why "But that's more than counterbalanced" (line 14) is an appropriate or effective link between the paragraph it begins and the previous one.

   2 A/E

5. Explain **in your own words** the **two** concerns of Professor Tom Sanders (line 15) about people's chocolate consumption.

   2 U

6. Why is it "good news" (line 25) that manufacturers are considering reducing the amount of fatty acids in their products?

   1 U

7. Explain fully why "Ironically" (line 27) is an appropriate choice of word at this point in the passage.

   3 A/E

8. (*a*) Look at the advertisement placed by John Cadbury (lines 30–32). Comment on the **word choice** or **tone**.

   1 A

   (*b*) "The nutritious link was one that early chocolate marketing followed." (line 33)

   Write down an expression from the rest of this paragraph, apart from "nutrition" or "nourish", which continues the idea of nourishment.

   1 U

9. Explain how effective "gatekeepers" (line 41) is as an image or metaphor.

   2 E

10. (*a*) How does the writer's **word choice** in the sentence beginning "Out went" (line 43) make clear to the reader the changing role of women in society?

    2 U/A

    (*b*) How does the **structure** of this sentence reinforce this idea of change?

    2 A

11. Explain fully why the word "fantasies" (line 47) is appropriate to describe the ideas behind the Flake advertisement.

    2 A

12. Look at the expression "kicked out". (line 49)

    Suggest **two** things this implies about the way people in the advertising industry conduct their business.

    2 U/A

13. There are "different types of chocolate being developed". (line 56)

    Explain **in your own words two** ways in which these new products would help consumers to think that "it's OK to eat some chocolate". (line 54)

    2 U

14. "Watch out for the Wagon Wheel." (line 63)

    (*a*) What can you deduce about what the Wagon Wheel was?

    1 U

    (*b*) Give **two** reasons why this sentence might be an effective advertising slogan.

    2 A/E

Total (30)

[END OF QUESTION PAPER]

X115/202

NATIONAL
QUALIFICATIONS
2006

FRIDAY, 12 MAY
2.20 PM – 3.50 PM

ENGLISH
INTERMEDIATE 2
Critical Essay

Answer **two** questions.

Each question must be taken from a different section.

Each question is worth 25 marks.

SCOTTISH
QUALIFICATIONS
AUTHORITY

Answer TWO questions from this paper.

Each question must be chosen from a different Section (A–E). You are not allowed to choose two questions from the same Section.

In all Sections you may use Scottish texts.

Write the number of each question in the margin of your answer booklet and begin each essay on a fresh page.

You should spend about 45 minutes on each essay.

The following will be assessed:

- **the relevance of your essays to the questions you have chosen**
- **your knowledge and understanding of key elements, central concerns and significant details of the chosen texts**
- **your explanation of ways in which aspects of structure/style/language contribute to the meaning/effect/impact of the chosen texts**
- **your evaluation of the effectiveness of the chosen texts, supported by detailed and relevant evidence**
- **the quality and technical accuracy of your writing.**

Each question is worth 25 marks. The total for this paper is 50 marks.

SECTION A—DRAMA

Answers to questions in this section should refer to the text and to such relevant features as: characterisation, key scene(s), structure, climax, theme, plot, conflict, setting . . .

1. Choose a play in which a character loses the support of her/his friends or family during the course of the play.

   What reasons are there for this loss of support and what effect does this lack of support have on the character's fate in the play?

2. Choose a play which you feel has a memorable opening scene or section.

   Show how the content or atmosphere of the scene or section provides an effective starting point for the development of the characters and the theme of the play.

3. Choose a play in which a character hides the truth from other characters in the play.

   State what the character hides and show how the revealing of the truth affects the outcome of the play.

SECTION B—PROSE

Answers to questions in this section should refer to the text and to such relevant features as: characterisation, setting, language, key incident(s), climax/turning point, plot, structure, narrative technique, theme, ideas, description . . .

4. Choose a novel **or** short story which deals with an important human issue: for example, poverty, war, family conflict, injustice, or any other issue you regard as important.

   State what the issue is and show how the characters cope with the issue in the course of the novel or short story.

5. Choose a novel **or** short story in which the main character makes an important decision.

   Explain why a decision is necessary and go on to show how the decision affects the rest of the novel or short story.

6. Choose a non-fiction text or group of texts which presents you with an interesting place **or** topic.

   Briefly identify the place or topic and go on to show how the writer's presentation made this interesting to you.

SECTION C—POETRY

Answers to questions in this section should refer to the text and to such relevant features as: word choice, tone, imagery, structure, content, rhythm, theme, sound, ideas . . .

7. Choose a poem which deals with birth **or** death **or** love **or** hate **or** jealousy.

   By looking at the content and language of the poem show how your understanding of one of these topics is deepened by your reading of the poem.

8. Choose a poem which deals with nature or the natural world.

   State what aspect of nature is being described and show how the use of poetic techniques deepens your understanding and appreciation of the topic.

9. Choose a poem which arouses strong emotion in you.

   State what it is about the subject of the poem which makes you feel strongly, and go on to show how the poet's use of language reinforces these feelings.

[Turn over

SECTION D—FILM AND TV DRAMA

Answers to questions in this section should refer to the text and to such relevant features as: use of camera, key sequence, characterisation, mise-en-scène, editing, setting, music/sound effects, plot, dialogue . . .

10. Choose a film which has a child or young person as its main character.

    Show how the character is introduced in the film in such a way that you realise he/she is important.

11. Choose a film or TV drama* which raises awareness of an important social issue.

    Identify the issue and show how its importance is brought home to you through the characters who convey these ideas to you.

12. Choose a film or TV drama* which involves conflict between two groups of people.

    Explain the reasons for the conflict and show how the portrayal of the conflict is highlighted by the use of media techniques.

    * "TV drama" includes a single play, a series or a serial.

SECTION E—LANGUAGE

Answers to questions in this section should refer to the text and to such relevant features as: register, accent, dialect, slang, jargon, vocabulary, tone, abbreviation . . .

13. Consider the use of persuasive language in the field of politics, **or** charitable campaigns, **or** commercial advertising.
    Show how the language tries to persuade you and discuss how successful it is in its aim.

14. Consider the differences in spoken language between two groups—for example, the inhabitants of different areas.

    Analyse the main differences between the ways of speaking of these groups and consider reasons for the differences.

15. Consider the special language associated with a particular job, hobby or sport.

    By giving examples show how the specialist language differs from non-specialist language and say what advantage is gained by the use of specialist language within the group which uses it.

[END OF QUESTION PAPER]

[BLANK PAGE]

X115/201

NATIONAL	FRIDAY, 11 MAY	ENGLISH
QUALIFICATIONS	1.00 PM – 2.00 PM	INTERMEDIATE 2
2007		Close Reading

Answer all questions.

30 marks are allocated to this paper.

Read the passage carefully and then answer **all** the questions, **using your own words as far as possible**.

The questions will ask you to show that:

you understand the main ideas and important details in the passage—in other words, **what** the writer has said (**Understanding—U**);

you can identify, using appropriate terms, the techniques the writer has used to get across these ideas—in other words, **how** he has said it (**Analysis—A**);

you can, using appropriate evidence, comment on how effective the writer has been—in other words, **how well** he has said it (**Evaluation—E**).

A code letter (U, A, E) is used alongside each question to identify its purpose for you. The number of marks attached to each question will give some indication of the length of answer required.

SCOTTISH QUALIFICATIONS AUTHORITY

Come fly with me

In this passage, the writer reflects on his fascination with birds and flight.

I was going through Monken Hadley churchyard and there were lots (note scientific precision) of house martins whizzing round the church tower. House martins are dapper little chaps, navy blue with white, and they are one of the sights of the summer: doing things like whizzing round church steeples and catching flies in their beaks. Later in the
5 season the young ones take up whizzing themselves, trying to get the hang of this flying business. So I paused on my journey to spend a few moments gazing at the whirligig of martins. It was nothing special, nothing exceptional, and it was very good indeed. Note this: one of the greatest pleasures of birdwatching is the quiet enjoyment of the absolutely ordinary.

10 And then it happened. Bam!

Gone.

From the tail of my eye, I saw what I took to be a kestrel. I turned my head to watch it as it climbed, and I waited for it to go into its hover, according to time-honoured kestrel custom. But it did nothing of the kind. It turned itself into an anchor. Or a
15 thunderbolt.

No kestrel this: it crashed into the crowd of martins, and almost as swiftly vanished. I think it got one, but I can't swear to it, it was all so fast.

It was a hobby-hawk. Perhaps the most dashing falcon of them all: slim, elegant and deadly fast. Not rare as rare-bird-addicts reckon things: they come to Britain in
20 reasonable numbers every summer to breed. The sight of a hobby-hawk makes no headlines in the birdwatching world. It was just a wonderful and wholly unexpected sight of a wonderful and wholly unexpected bird. It was a moment of perfect drama.

Birdwatching is a state of being, not an activity. It doesn't depend on place, on equipment, on specific purpose, like, say, fishing. It is not a matter of organic
25 trainspotting; it is about life and it is about living. It is a matter of keeping the eyes and ears and mind open. It is not a matter of obsession, not at all. It is just quiet enjoyment.

Flight is the dream of every human being. When we are lucky, we do, quite literally, dream about flying. They are the best of all dreams—you are free, you are miraculous.

The desire to fly is part of the condition of being human. That's why most of the
30 non-confrontational sports are about flying, or at least the defiance of gravity. Gymnastics is about the power of the human body to fly unaided; so is the high jump and the long jump. The throwing events—discus, shot-put and hammer—are about making something else fly: a war on gravity.

Golf always seems to me a trivial game, but every one of its legion of addicts will tell you
35 that it all comes back to the pure joy of a clean strike at the ball: making it defy gravity. Making it climb like a towering snipe. Making it soar like an eagle, at least in the mind of the striker, as it reaches the top of its long, graceful parabola.

Think about it: all these sports are done for the joy of flying. Skating is a victory over friction, and it feels like victory over gravity; it feels like flying. Its antithesis is
40 weightlifting: a huge and brutal event, the idea of which is to beat gravity. All the horsey events come back to the idea of flight: of getting off the ground, of escaping human limitations by joining up with another species and finding flight. For every rider, every horse has wings.

And birds fly in all kinds of ways: the brisk purpose of a sparrow, the airy detachment of
45 the seagull, the dramatic power of the hawk. Some birds specialise in flying very fast;
others in flying very slow. Great hunters such as the barn owl work on the edge of the
stall all the time. Kestrels are very good at flying without moving at all. Some birds are
not so great at flying. Pheasants just about get off the ground into a safe place in a tree
for a night. They are poor flyers, but they are unquestionably better than us humans.

50 And flight attracts our eyes, lifts our heart with joy and envy. Flight, to us earthbound
creatures, is a form of magic—one of the great powers attributed to decent wizards and
witches throughout history is the ability to fly, from the persecuted sorcerers of the Dark
Ages to the players of the game of quidditch.

Take a basic urban moment—a traffic jam, a train becalmed. A sigh, a look away from
55 the road or the newspaper, out of the window. A skein of geese in the sky; probably,
almost certainly, "just" Canada geese. Too far away to hear them honking to each other,
urgent instructions to keep the formation tight and to help the leader out with the hard
work. A daily sight, a common sight, an ordinary sight. But just for one
second—perhaps even two—you are let off the day's hassles. At least that is the case if
60 you take the trouble to look up. It will probably be the most inspiring thing you will see
all day. The day is the better for those birds.

And so we look to birds for a deep-seated kind of joy. It goes back to the dawn of
humankind: ever since humans first walked upright, they were able to turn their eyes to
the heavens and observe the birds. The birds have something we can never have. But
65 merely by existing—by flying before us—they add to the daily joys of existence. Birds
are about hope.

Adapted from *How to be a Bad Birdwatcher* by Simon Barnes

QUESTIONS   *Marks Code*

1. Explain what is odd or ironic about the expression "note scientific precision" (lines 1–2).   2   A

2. "It was nothing special, nothing exceptional, and it was very good indeed." (line 7).

   (*a*) What is surprising about this statement?   1   A

   (*b*) Show how the writer continues this idea in the next sentence (lines 8–9). 2   U/A

3. Identify **two** techniques used in lines 10 and 11 which help to convey the idea of speed described in the next two paragraphs (lines 12–17).   2   A

4. (*a*) What is the author suggesting about the bird when he says "It turned itself into an anchor" (line 14)?   1   U/A

   (*b*) Why is the comparison of the bird to a "thunderbolt" (line 15) an effective image or metaphor?   2   E

5. Explain with clear reference to the whole sentence why the writer uses a colon in line 19.   2   A

6. "The sight of a hobby-hawk makes no headlines in the birdwatching world" (lines 20–21). Explain **in your own words** what is meant by "makes no headlines".   1   U

7. Write down the word from later in the paragraph which continues the idea introduced by "trainspotting" (line 25).   1   U

8. In what way does the author's use of "quite literally" (line 27) help to make his meaning clear?   1   U/A

9. (*a*) What does "trivial" (line 34) tell us about the writer's attitude to golf? 1   U

   (*b*) Explain how an expression later in this sentence makes it clear that the author is aware that others do not share his opinion.   2   U/A

   (*c*) Why are the comparisons the writer uses in the rest of this paragraph appropriate?   2   A/E

10. The writer mentions a variety of sports between lines 29 and 43. What challenge does he think these activities have in common?   1   U

11. The writer refers to equestrianism ("horsey events", line 41), as related to the pursuit of flight. What is the difference between this and all the other sports he mentions? Answer **in your own words**.   1   U

12. Why is it appropriate to introduce the paragraph consisting of lines 44 to 49 with the expression "And birds fly in all kinds of ways"?   2   A/E

13. The writer refers to "wizards and witches throughout history" (lines 51–52). Explain by referring to either **word choice** or **structure** how the rest of the sentence continues this idea.   2   U/A

14. What do the writer's examples of "a basic urban moment" (line 54) have in common?   1   U

15. What is the effect of the inverted commas round "just" in line 56?   1   A

16. Explain fully why the last paragraph (lines 62–66) provides an appropriate or effective conclusion to the passage.   2   E

[END OF QUESTION PAPER]   **Total (30)**

X115/202

NATIONAL
QUALIFICATIONS
2007

FRIDAY, 11 MAY
2.20 PM – 3.50 PM

ENGLISH
INTERMEDIATE 2
Critical Essay

Answer **two** questions.

Each question must be taken from a different section.

Each question is worth 25 marks.

Answer TWO questions from this paper.

Each question must be chosen from a different Section (A–E). You are not allowed to choose two questions from the same Section.

In all Sections you may use Scottish texts.

Write the number of each question in the margin of your answer booklet and begin each essay on a fresh page.

You should spend about 45 minutes on each essay.

The following will be assessed:

- **the relevance of your essays to the questions you have chosen**

- **your knowledge and understanding of key elements, central concerns and significant details of the chosen texts**

- **your explanation of ways in which aspects of structure/style/language contribute to the meaning/effect/impact of the chosen texts**

- **your evaluation of the effectiveness of the chosen texts, supported by detailed and relevant evidence**

- **the quality and technical accuracy of your writing.**

Each question is worth 25 marks. The total for this paper is 50 marks.

SECTION A—DRAMA

Answers to questions in this section should refer to the text and to such relevant features as: characterisation, key scene(s), structure, climax, theme, plot, conflict, setting . . .

1. Choose a play which portrays a strong relationship between two of the main characters.

   Describe the nature of the relationship and explain how the relationship influences the fate of the two characters concerned.

2. Choose a play in which there is a highly emotional scene.

   Show how this scene increases your understanding of the characters involved and how it is important in the unfolding of the plot of the play.

3. Choose a play which has, as a central concern, an issue which is of importance in today's society.

   State what the issue is and show how the playwright's handling of the plot and characters increases your understanding of the issue.

SECTION B—PROSE

Answers to questions in this section should refer to the text and to such relevant features as: characterisation, setting, language, key incident(s), climax/turning point, plot, structure, narrative technique, theme, ideas, description . . .

4. Choose a novel **or** short story in which **two** of the main characters have a disagreement which is important to the outcome of the novel or short story.

   Identify the reasons for the disagreement and go on to show how the effects of the disagreement have an impact on the rest of the novel or short story.

5. Choose a prose text (fiction or non-fiction) in which a society **or** a person **or** a culture **or** a setting is effectively portrayed.

   Show how the writer's presentation of the subject makes an impact on you, and helps you to understand the subject in greater depth.

6. Choose a novel **or** short story which has a striking opening.

   Show how the opening is effective in introducing the character(s) **and/or** the atmosphere **and/or** the setting.

SECTION C—POETRY

Answers to questions in this section should refer to the text and to such relevant features as: word choice, tone, imagery, structure, content, rhythm, theme, sound, ideas . . .

7. Choose a poem which seems to be about an ordinary everyday experience but which actually makes a deeper comment about life.

   Explain what the poem is about and go on to show how the techniques used by the poet help to make the ideas memorable.

8. Choose a poem which creates pity or sympathy in you.

   Show how the feelings of pity or sympathy are brought into focus by the use of poetic techniques.

9. Choose a poem which describes a scene or incident vividly.

   Briefly state what is being described and then go on to show how the poetic techniques used make the description vivid.

[Turn over

SECTION D—FILM AND TV DRAMA

Answers to questions in this section should refer to the text and to such relevant features as: use of camera, key sequence, characterisation, mise-en-scène, editing, setting, music/sound effects, plot, dialogue . . .

10. Choose a film or TV drama* which creates suspense or tension either in a particular scene **or** throughout the whole film or TV drama.

    Show how the suspense or tension is created and how it affects your enjoyment of the film or TV drama* as a whole.

11. Choose a film or TV drama* which deals with crime **or** espionage **or** detection.

    Show how the film or TV drama* captures and holds your interest by its choice of content and use of media techniques.

12. Choose a film or TV drama* which depends to some extent on humour to make an impact.

    Briefly state what you consider to be the humorous aspects of the film or TV drama* and go on to show how the film or programme makers use various techniques to create the humour.

    * "TV drama" includes a single play, a series or a serial.

SECTION E—LANGUAGE

Answers to questions in this section should refer to the text and to such relevant features as: register, accent, dialect, slang, jargon, vocabulary, tone, abbreviation . . .

13. Consider the aspects of language which make advertising effective.

    Choose two advertisements which you feel vary in their effectiveness. By looking closely at each advertisement explain why you felt that one was more effective than the other.

14. Consider the language of two groups of people who are different in some significant way. For example, they may be from different generations or different places.

    By looking at examples of the language of each group, describe the differences between the two, and discuss the advantages **and/or** disadvantages which might arise from the different ways of using language.

15. Consider a modern means of communication such as e-mailing or text-messaging.

    By referring to specific examples show what are the advantages and disadvantages of the method of communication which you have chosen.

[END OF QUESTION PAPER]

[BLANK PAGE]

X115/201

NATIONAL QUALIFICATIONS 2008	THURSDAY, 15 MAY 1.00 PM – 2.00 PM	ENGLISH INTERMEDIATE 2 Close Reading

Answer all questions.

30 marks are allocated to this paper.

Read the passage carefully and then answer **all** the questions, **using your own words as far as possible**.

The questions will ask you to show that:

you understand the main ideas and important details in the passage—in other words, **what** the writer has said (**Understanding—U**);

you can identify, using appropriate terms, the techniques the writer has used to get across these ideas—in other words, **how** he has said it (**Analysis—A**);

you can, using appropriate evidence, comment on how effective the writer has been—in other words, **how well** he has said it (**Evaluation—E**).

A code letter (U, A, E) is used alongside each question to identify its purpose for you. The number of marks attached to each question will give some indication of the length of answer required.

Afar, far away

Matthew Parris describes the harsh conditions of life in North Africa, and suggests what may be in store for the region and the nomadic (wandering) people who live there.

At the beginning of this month I was in a hellish yet beautiful place. I was making a programme for Radio 4 about one of the world's most ancient trade routes. Every year, since (we suppose) at least the time of the Ancient Greeks, hundreds of thousands of camels are led, strung together in trains, from the highlands of Ethiopia into the Danakil
5 depression: a descent into the desert of nearly 10,000 feet, a journey of about 100 miles. Here, by the edge of a blue-black and bitter salt lake, great floes of rock salt encrusting the mud are prised up, hacked into slabs and loaded on to the camels.

Then the camels and their drivers make the climb through dry mountains back into the highlands, where the slabs are bound with tape and distributed across the Horn of
10 Africa. The camels drink only twice on their journey, walking often at night, and carrying with them straw to eat on the way back. Their drivers bring only dry bread, sugar and tea.

Travelling with the camel trains in mid-winter, when temperatures are bearable, I found the experience extraordinarily moving. But my thoughts went beyond the salt trade, and
15 were powerfully reinforced by the journey that followed it—to another desert, the Algerian Sahara.

These reflections were first prompted by a chance remark that could not have been more wrong. Our superb Ethiopian guide, Solomon Berhe, was sitting with me in a friendly but flyblown village of sticks, stones, cardboard and tin in Hamed Ela, 300ft below sea
20 level, in a hot wind, on a hot night. An infinity of stars blazed above. The mysterious lake was close, and when the wind changed you could smell the sulphur blowing from a range of bubbling vents of gas, salt and super-heated steam. On the horizon fumed the volcano, Hertale. With not a blade of grass in sight, and all around us a desert of black rocks, the Danakil is a kind of inferno. How the Afar people manage to live in
25 this place, and why they choose to, puzzles the rest of Ethiopia, as it does me.

"But," said Solomon, scratching one of the small fly-bites that were troubling all of us, "if we could return here in 50 years, this village would be different. There will be streets, electricity, and proper buildings. As Ethiopia modernises, places like this will be made more comfortable for people. Hamed Ela will probably be a big town."

30 And that is where Solomon was wrong. As Ethiopia modernises, the Afar will leave their desert home. They will drift into the towns and cities in the highlands. Their voracious herds of goats will die. Their camels will no longer be of any use. The only remembrance this place will have of the humans it bred will be the stone fittings of their flimsy, ruined stick huts, and the mysterious black rock burial mounds that litter the
35 landscape.

There is no modern reason for human beings to live in such places. Their produce is pitiful, the climate brutal and the distances immense. Salt is already produced as cheaply by industrial means. If market forces don't kill the trade, the conscience of the animal rights movement will, for the laden camels suffer horribly on their journey. The
40 day is coming when camels will go down there no more. In fifty years the Danakil will be a national park, visited by rubbernecking tourists in helicopters. Camels will be found in zoos. Goats will be on their way to elimination from every ecologically fragile part of the planet.

Even in America, deserts are not properly inhabited any more. Unreal places such as
45 Las Vegas have sprung up where people live in an air-conditioned and artificially
irrigated bubble, but the land itself is emptier than before. Tribes who were part of the
land, and lived off it, have mostly gone, their descendants living in reservations. The
wilderness places of North America are vast and exceptionally well preserved; but they
are not part of many people's lives, except those of tourists. We are becoming outsiders
50 to the natural world, watching it on the Discovery Channel.

Those who call themselves environmentalists celebrate this. "Leave nothing and take
nothing away," read the signs at the gates of nature reserves. Practical advice, perhaps,
but is there not something melancholy in what that says about modern man's desired
relationship with nature? Will we one day confine ourselves to watching large parts of
55 our planet only from observation towers?

I have no argument against the international development movement that wants to see
the Afars in clean houses with running water and electrical power, and schools, and a
clinic nearby—away, in other words, from their gruesome desert life. All this is
inevitable.

60 But as that new way of living arrives—as we retreat from the wild places, and the fences
of national parks go up; as we cease the exploitation of animals, and the cow, the camel,
the sheep, the chicken and the pig become items in modern exhibition farms, where
schoolchildren see how mankind used to live; as our direct contact with our fellow
creatures is restricted to zoos, pets and fish tanks; and as every area of natural beauty is
65 set about with preservation orders and rules to keep human interference to a
minimum—will we not be separating ourselves from our planet in order, as we suppose,
to look after it better? Will we not be loving nature, but leaving it?

They say there is less traffic across the Sahara today than at any time in human history,
even if you include motor transport. The great days of camel caravans are over. As for
70 the inhabitants, the nomads are on a path to extinction as a culture. Nomadic life does
not fit the pattern of nation states, taxes, frontiers and controls. And though for them
there is now government encouragement to stay, their culture is doomed. Amid the
indescribable majesty of this place—the crumbling towers of black rock, the scream of
the jackal, the waterless canyons, yellow dunes, grey plateaus and purple thorn
75 bushes—I have felt like a visitor to a monumental ruin, walked by ghosts. There are
fragments of pottery, thousands of cave paintings of deer, giraffe, elephant, and men in
feathers, dancing . . . but no people, not a soul.

In the beginning, man is expelled from the Garden of Eden. In the end, perhaps, we
shall leave it of our own accord, closing the gate behind us.

From *The Times,* February 25, 2006 (slightly adapted)

QUESTIONS   *Marks Code*

1. What is surprising about the writer's **word choice** in the first sentence?   2   A

2. Why does the writer add the expression "we suppose" (line 3) to the sentence here?   1   U

3. The word "floes" (line 6) usually refers to icebergs.

   Explain how it is appropriate to use it as a metaphor to refer to the appearance of the rock salt deposits.   2   A/E

4. Explain how any **one** example of the writer's choice of descriptive detail in lines 10–12 emphasises the hardships of the journey.   1   A

5. Explain **in your own words** the contrasting impressions the writer has of the village in Hamed Ela (see lines 18–19).   2   U

6. Explain what the word "fumed" (line 22) suggests about the volcano, apart from having smoke coming from it.   1   U

7. Explain why the sentence "And that is where Solomon was wrong" (line 30) is an effective link between the paragraphs contained in lines 26 to 35.   2   E

8. What does the word "drift" suggest about how "the Afar will leave their desert home" (lines 30 –31)?   1   U

9. The writer tells us "There is no modern reason for human beings to live in such places" (line 36).

   Explain **in your own words two** reasons why this is the case.

   Look in the next three sentences (lines 36–39) for your answer.   2   U

10. Explain fully the appropriateness of the **word choice** of "rubbernecking tourists in helicopters" (line 41).   2   A

11. Explain how the writer develops the idea of Las Vegas being "Unreal" (line 44).   2   A

12. Explain why the expression "watching it on the Discovery Channel" (line 50) effectively illustrates our relationship with "wilderness places".   2   E

13. What is the effect of the writer's inclusion of the words "Those who call themselves" in the sentence beginning in line 51?   1   U

14. What is the **tone** of the two sentences in lines 52–55?   1   A

15. Explain how other words in lines 56–58 help us to work out the meaning or sense of "gruesome desert life".   2   U

16. Look at lines 60–67.

    (*a*) Identify any feature of **sentence structure** the writer uses effectively in this paragraph.   1   A

    (*b*) Show how your chosen feature helps to clarify or support the writer's argument.   2   A

17. Explain **in your own words** why "the nomads are on a path to extinction as a culture" (line 70).   1   U

18. Explain any reason why the final paragraph (lines 78–79) works well as a conclusion to the passage.   2   E

Total (30)

[END OF QUESTION PAPER]

X115/202

NATIONAL
QUALIFICATIONS
2008

THURSDAY, 15 MAY
2.20 PM – 3.50 PM

ENGLISH
INTERMEDIATE 2
Critical Essay

Answer **two** questions.

Each question must be taken from a different section.

Each question is worth 25 marks.

Answer TWO questions from this paper.

Each question must be chosen from a different Section (A–E). You are not allowed to choose two questions from the same Section.

In all Sections you may use Scottish texts.

Write the number of each question in the margin of your answer booklet and begin each essay on a fresh page.

You should spend about 45 minutes on each essay.

The following will be assessed:

- **the relevance of your essays to the questions you have chosen**

- **your knowledge and understanding of key elements, central concerns and significant details of the chosen texts**

- **your explanation of ways in which aspects of structure/style/language contribute to the meaning/effect/impact of the chosen texts**

- **your evaluation of the effectiveness of the chosen texts, supported by detailed and relevant evidence**

- **the quality and technical accuracy of your writing.**

Each question is worth 25 marks. The total for this paper is 50 marks.

SECTION A—DRAMA

Answers to questions in this section should refer to the text and to such relevant features as: characterisation, key scene(s), structure, climax, theme, plot, conflict, setting . . .

1. Choose a play in which there is a significant conflict between two characters.

   Describe the conflict and show how it is important to the development of the characterisation and theme of the play.

2. Choose a play which has a tragic ending.

   Show how the ending of the play results from the strengths and/or weaknesses of the main character(s).

3. Choose a play in which a character encounters difficulties within the community in which he or she lives.

   Show how the character copes with the difficulties he or she encounters and how his or her actions contribute to the theme of the play.

SECTION B—PROSE

Answers to questions in this section should refer to the text and to such relevant features as: characterisation, setting, language, key incident(s), climax/turning point, plot, structure, narrative technique, theme, ideas, description . . .

4. Choose a novel **or** short story which has a turning point or moment of realisation for at least one of the characters.

   Briefly describe what has led up to the turning point or moment. Go on to show what impact this has on the character(s) and how it affects the outcome of the novel or story.

5. Choose a novel **or** short story in which you feel sympathy with one of the main characters because of the difficulties or injustice or hardships she or he has to face.

   Describe the problems the character faces and show by what means you are made to feel sympathy for her or him.

6. Choose a non-fiction text **or** group of texts which uses setting, **or** humour, **or** description to make clear to you an interesting aspect of a society.

   Show how the use of any of these techniques helped you to understand the writer's point of view on the interesting aspect of this society.

SECTION C—POETRY

Answers to questions in this section should refer to the text and to such relevant features as: word choice, tone, imagery, structure, content, rhythm, theme, sound, ideas . . .

7. Choose a poem which creates an atmosphere of sadness, pity, or loss.

   Show how the poet creates the atmosphere and what effect it has on your response to the subject matter of the poem.

8. Choose a poem about a strong relationship—for example, between two people, or between a person and a place.

   Show how the poet, by the choice of content and the skilful use of techniques, helps you to appreciate the strength of the relationship.

9. Choose a poem which reflects on an aspect of human behaviour in such a way as to deepen your understanding of human nature.

   Describe the aspect of human behaviour which you have identified and show how the poet's use of ideas and techniques brought you to a deeper understanding of human nature.

[Turn over

SECTION D—FILM AND TV DRAMA

> *Answers to questions in this section should refer to the text and to such relevant features as: use of camera, key sequence, characterisation, mise-en-scène, editing, setting, music/sound effects, plot, dialogue . . .*

10. Choose a film or TV drama* which involves the pursuit of power or the fulfilment of an ambition.

    Show how the theme is developed through the presentation of character and setting.

11. Choose an opening sequence from a film which effectively holds your interest and makes you want to watch the rest of the film.

    Show what elements of the opening sequence have this effect, and how they relate to the film as a whole.

12. Choose a film or TV drama* which reflects an important aspect of society.

    Describe the aspect of society being dealt with and show how the techniques used by the film or programme maker help to deepen your understanding of the importance of this aspect.

* "TV drama" includes a single play, a series or a serial.

SECTION E—LANGUAGE

> *Answers to questions in this section should refer to the text and to such relevant features as: register, accent, dialect, slang, jargon, vocabulary, tone, abbreviation . . .*

13. Consider the language of advertising.

    In any one advertisement identify the ways in which language is used successfully. Explain what it is about these usages which makes them effective.

14. Consider the language of any form of modern electronic communication.

    Identify some features of this language which differ from normal usage and say how effective you think these features are in communicating information.

15. Consider the distinctive language of any specific group of people.

    What aspects of the group's language are distinctive and what advantage does the group gain from the use of such language?

[END OF QUESTION PAPER]

English Intermediate 2
Critical Essay 2005

Marking principles for Critical Essay are as follows

- Each essay should first be read to establish whether the essay achieves success in **all** the Performance Criteria for Grade C, including relevance and the standards for technical accuracy outlined in Note 1 below.

- If minimum standards are not achieved in any **one** or more of the Performance Criteria, the maximum mark which can be awarded is 11.

- If minimum standards have been achieved, then the supplementary marking grids will allow you to place the work on a scale of marks out of 25.

- The Category awarded and the mark should be placed at the end of the essay.

Notes

1. "Sufficiently accurate" can best be defined in terms of a definition of "consistently accurate".

   - *Consistently accurate*
     A few errors may be present, but these will not be significant in any way. The candidate may use some complex vocabulary and sentence structures. Where appropriate, sentences will show accurate handling of clauses. Linking between sentences will be clear. Paragraphing will reflect a developing line of thought.

   - *Sufficiently accurate*
     As above but with an allowance made for speed and the lack of opportunity to redraft.

2. Using the Category descriptions

   - Categories are not grades. Although derived from performance criteria at C and the indicators of excellence for Grade A, the four categories are designed primarily to assist with placing each candidate response at an appropriate point on a continuum of achievement. Assumptions about final grades or association of final grades with particular categories should not be allowed to influence objective assessment.

   - Once an essay has been deemed to pass the basic criteria, it does not have to meet all the suggestions for Category II (for example) to fall into that Category. More typically there will be a spectrum of strengths and weaknesses which span categories.

Grade C
Performance Criteria

(a) *Understanding*
As appropriate to task, the response demonstrates understanding of key elements, central concerns and significant details of the text(s).

(b) *Analysis*
The response explains in some detail ways in which aspects of structure/style/language contribute to meaning/effect/impact.

(c) *Evaluation*
The response reveals engagement with the text(s) or aspects of the text(s) and stated or implied evaluation of effectiveness, substantiated by some relevant evidence from the text(s).

(d) *Expression*
Structure, style and language, including use of some appropriate critical terminology, are deployed to communicate meaning clearly and develop a line of thought which is generally relevant to purpose; spelling, grammar and punctuation are sufficiently accurate.

It should be noted that the term "text" encompasses printed, audio or film/video text(s) which may be literary (fiction or non-fiction) or may relate to aspects of media or language.

Language Questions 13-15

- The "text" which should be dealt with in a language question is the research which the pupil has done. Examples taken from their research must be there for you to see.

- However, to demonstrate understanding and analysis related to these examples there has to be some ability to generalise from the particular, to classify and comment on what has been discovered. It is not enough merely to produce a list of words in, say, Dundonian with their standard English equivalents. This is merely description and without any further development does not demonstrate understanding of any principle underlying the choice of words.

- The list of features offered to the candidate in each question is supportive. There may be others, but one would expect some of those mentioned would be dealt with.

English Intermediate 2
Critical Essay 2005 (continued)

Intermediate 2 Critical Essay Supplementary Advice

This advice, which is supplementary to the published Performance Criteria, is designed to assist with the placing of scripts within the full range of marks. However, the Performance Criteria as published give the primary definitions. The mark range for each Category is identified.

IV 8–11	III 12–15	II 16–19	I 20–25
• An essay which falls into this category may do so for a variety of reasons. It could be • that it fails to achieve sufficient technical accuracy • or that any knowledge and understanding of the material is not deployed as a response relevant to the task • or that analysis and evaluation attempted are unconvincing • or that the answer is simply too thin.	**Understanding** • Knowledge of the text(s), and a basic understanding of the **main** concerns will be used .... to provide an answer which is **generally relevant** to the task.	**Understanding** • Knowledge and understanding of the **central** concerns of the text(s) will be used .... to provide an answer which is **mainly relevant** to the task.	**Understanding** • **Secure** knowledge **and some insight** into the central concerns of the text(s) will be demonstrated at this level .... and there will be a line of thought **consistently relevant** to the task.
	• Some reference to the text(s) will be made to **support** the candidate's argument.	• Reference to the text(s) will be used as evidence to **promote** the candidate's argument.	• Reference to the text(s) will be used **appropriately** as evidence which helps to **develop** the argument **fully**.
	Analysis • There will be an **explanation** of the contribution of literary/linguistic techniques to the impact of the text(s).	**Analysis** • There will be an **explanation of the effectiveness** of the contribution of literary/linguistic techniques to the impact of the text(s).	**Analysis** • There will be **some insight** shown into the **effectiveness** of the contribution of literary/linguistic techniques to the impact of the text(s).
	Evaluation • There will be **some engagement** with the text(s) which will state or imply an evaluation of its effectiveness.	**Evaluation** • There will be **engagement** with the text(s) which leads to a **generally valid** evaluative stance with respect to the text(s).	**Evaluation** • There will be a **clear engagement** with the text(s) which leads to a **valid** evaluative stance with respect to the material.
	Expression • Language will communicate the argument clearly, and there will be appropriate critical terminology deployed. Spelling, grammar and punctuation will be sufficiently accurate.	**Expression** • Language will communicate the argument **clearly**, and there will be appropriate critical terminology deployed **to aid the argument**. Spelling, grammar and punctuation will be sufficiently accurate.	**Expression** • The language will communicate **effectively** making appropriate use of critical terminology **to further the argument**. Spelling, grammar and punctuation will be sufficiently accurate.

English Intermediate 2
Close Reading 2006

1. it has been successful/popular/sought after etc

2. *Any one appropriate quotation and comment from e.g.:*
   - unlikelihood/anachronism of placing together of Aztec and advertising executive;
   - tongue-in-cheek/cynical tone of "beguile" or "essential part of our life";
   - contrast between "muddy brown discovery" and "food of the gods";
   - reductive/belittling nature of expression "fat, sugar and a type of caffeine";
   - excess/stereotyping of "excitedly branding";
   - exaggeration in "food of the gods"

3. *Any two of:*
   - pleasant texture/melting quality (gloss of "dissolve-in-the-mouth feeling" or "melts just below body temperature");
   - ability to give (immediate) boost or stimulation (gloss of "sudden charge of energy" or "the kick of the caffeine");
   - improvement in temper/attitude/feelings (gloss of "mood enhancer");
   - counteracts illness/hypertension (gloss of "cure for all ills" or "help high blood pressure");
   - less damaging to teeth (gloss of "doesn't have the teeth-rotting qualities of other sweets")

4. gives the idea of diversion from perceived virtues mentioned in previous paragraph (anti-hypertensive quality and/or absence of damaging effect on teeth) to indication of less desirable/unhealthy ingredients (fats and sugars)

5. *Any two of:*
   people eating more than/nearly twice as much as they divulge/confess/declare (gloss of "admit"); larger size/proportions/dimensions of products (gloss of "super-size"); content of chocolate bars

6. they are related to (heart) disease OR this is in line with (Government) advice
   (Lifts acceptable)

7. it is incongruous/curious/funny/wry/odd/paradoxical that chocolate is now giving concern about health when it was originally sold as being health-promoting/good for us

8. (a) *word choice:*
   anachronistic/old-fashioned diction OR formal register
   tone:
   (surprisingly) polite/deferential/formal

   (b) *Any of:*
   "keep them going"
   "energise"
   "sustain"
   "whole meal"

9. Appropriate because:
   idea(s) of responsibility/protecting/refusing or allowing admission match(es) their role in family life/what they do and do not purchase

10. (a) "stoic" OR "meal on the run" contrasts with/is different from "Me" OR "(sense of) indulgence"

    (b) balance/contrast of "Out/went ... in/came" (single words acceptable)

11. *Any two of:*
    - they are imaginary/unrealistic
    - they are pleasurable
    - they are self-generated

12. *Any two of:*
    - they readily embrace change;
    - they are ruthless in their habits;
    - they lack sentiment or involvement

13. *Any two of:*
    - they are less fattening/contain fewer nutrients (gloss of "low calorie bars");
    - they are less bulky/chunky (gloss of "lighter" or "monolithic-looking");
    - they encourage dividing/splitting (gloss of "shared (among friends)");
    - they have superior ingredients (gloss of "organic"/"exotic"/"high quality"

14. (a) it is an example of the "comforting chocolates you remember from your childhood"

    (b) *Any two of:*
    alliteration; pun/humour; brevity/snappiness; use of imperative verb; reference to idea of change

English Intermediate 2
Critical Essay 2006

Marking principles for Critical Essay are as follows

- Each essay should first be read to establish whether the essay achieves success in **all** the Performance Criteria for Grade C, including relevance and the standards for technical accuracy outlined in Note 1 below.

- If minimum standards are not achieved in any **one** or more of the Performance Criteria, the maximum mark which can be awarded is 11.

- If minimum standards have been achieved, then the supplementary marking grids will allow you to place the work on a scale of marks out of 25.

- The Category awarded and the mark should be placed at the end of the essay.

Notes

1. "Sufficiently accurate" can best be defined in terms of a definition of "consistently accurate".

    - *Consistently accurate*
      A few errors may be present, but these will not be significant in any way. The candidate may use some complex vocabulary and sentence structures. Where appropriate, sentences will show accurate handling of clauses. Linking between sentences will be clear. Paragraphing will reflect a developing line of thought.

    - *Sufficiently accurate*
      As above but with an allowance made for speed and the lack of opportunity to redraft.

2. Using the Category descriptions

    - Categories are not grades. Although derived from performance criteria at C and the indicators of excellence for Grade A, the four categories are designed primarily to assist with placing each candidate response at an appropriate point on a continuum of achievement. Assumptions about final grades or association of final grades with particular categories should not be allowed to influence objective assessment.

    - Once an essay has been deemed to pass the basic criteria, it does not have to meet all the suggestions for Category II (for example) to fall into that Category. More typically there will be a spectrum of strengths and weaknesses which span categories.

Grade C
Performance Criteria

(a) *Understanding*
     As appropriate to task, the response demonstrates understanding of key elements, central concerns and significant details of the text(s).

(b) *Analysis*
     The response explains in some detail ways in which aspects of structure/style/language contribute to meaning/effect/impact.

(c) *Evaluation*
     The response reveals engagement with the text(s) or aspects of the text(s) and stated or implied evaluation of effectiveness, substantiated by some relevant evidence from the text(s).

(d) *Expression*
     Structure, style and language, including use of some appropriate critical terminology, are deployed to communicate meaning clearly and develop a line of thought which is generally relevant to purpose; spelling, grammar and punctuation are sufficiently accurate.

It should be noted that the term "text" encompasses printed, audio or film/video text(s) which may be literary (fiction or non-fiction) or may relate to aspects of media or language.

Language Questions 13-15

- The "text" which should be dealt with in a language question is the research which the pupil has done. Examples taken from their research must be there for you to see.

- However, to demonstrate understanding and analysis related to these examples there has to be some ability to generalise from the particular, to classify and comment on what has been discovered. It is not enough merely to produce a list of words in, say, Dundonian with their standard English equivalents. This is merely description and without any further development does not demonstrate understanding of any principle underlying the choice of words.

- The list of features offered to the candidate in each question is supportive. There may be others, but one would expect some of those mentioned would be dealt with.

Intermediate 2 Critical Essay Supplementary Advice

This advice, which is supplementary to the published Performance Criteria, is designed to assist with the placing of scripts within the full range of marks. However, the Performance Criteria as published give the primary definitions. The mark range for each Category is identified.

IV 8–11	III 12–15	II 16–19	I 20–25
• An essay which falls into this category may do so for a variety of reasons. It could be • that it fails to achieve sufficient technical accuracy • or that any knowledge and understanding of the material is not deployed as a response relevant to the task • or that analysis and evaluation attempted are unconvincing • or that the answer is simply too thin.	**Understanding** • Knowledge of the text(s), and a basic understanding of the **main** concerns will be used .... to provide an answer which is **generally relevant** to the task. • Some reference to the text(s) will be made to **support** the candidate's argument.	**Understanding** • Knowledge and understanding of the **central** concerns of the text(s) will be used .... to provide an answer which is **mainly relevant** to the task. • Reference to the text(s) will be used as evidence to **promote** the candidate's argument.	**Understanding** • **Secure** knowledge **and some insight** into the central concerns of the text(s) will be demonstrated at this level .... and there will be a line of thought **consistently relevant** to the task. • Reference to the text(s) will be used **appropriately** as evidence which helps to **develop** the argument **fully**.
	Analysis • There will be an **explanation** of the contribution of literary/linguistic techniques to the impact of the text(s).	**Analysis** • There will be an **explanation of the effectiveness** of the contribution of literary/linguistic techniques to the impact of the text(s).	**Analysis** • There will be **some insight** shown into the **effectiveness** of the contribution of literary/linguistic techniques to the impact of the text(s).
	Evaluation • There will be **some engagement** with the text(s) which will state or imply an evaluation of its effectiveness.	**Evaluation** • There will be **engagement** with the text(s) which leads to a **generally valid** evaluative stance with respect to the text(s).	**Evaluation** • There will be a **clear engagement** with the text(s) which leads to a **valid** evaluative stance with respect to the material.
	Expression • Language will communicate the argument clearly, and there will be appropriate critical terminology deployed. Spelling, grammar and punctuation will be sufficiently accurate.	**Expression** • Language will communicate the argument **clearly**, and there will be appropriate critical terminology deployed **to aid the argument**. Spelling, grammar and punctuation will be sufficiently accurate.	**Expression** • The language will communicate **effectively** making appropriate use of critical terminology **to further the argument**. Spelling, grammar and punctuation will be sufficiently accurate.

English Intermediate 2
Close Reading 2007

1. The writer uses "lots" which is not precise/scientific.

2. (a) It is a paradox/(apparently) contradictory.

   (b) He repeats the idea of opposites in "greatest pleasures" and "(the) absolutely ordinary".

3. *Any two of*
   - Very short sentences
   - single word/very short paragraphs
   - colloquialism
   - monosyllable(s)
   - exclamation mark
   - (idea of) minor sentence
   - onomatopoeia.

4. (a) It changed its shape/resembled/adopted the shape of an anchor/looked like an anchor.
   OR
   It descended vertically/swiftly.

   (b) It suggests:
   Any two of
   - suddenness
   - destructiveness
   - coming from the sky
   - speed

5. "reasonable numbers" (following the colon) expands/explains
   the idea of their being "not rare".

6. It is an ordinary event/it is not newsworthy or unusual/no-one makes a fuss.

7. Obsession.

8. Points out that meaning is dreaming in the real sense/not figurative/not in the sense of wishing or imagining or aspiring.

9. (a) (He thinks) it is a waste of time/worthless/pointless/unimportant.

   (b) "legion" suggests it has many devotees
   OR
   "addicts" suggests (the intensity of) the hold of the game
   OR
   "pure joy" conveys (the intensity of) the pleasure of the game'.

   (c) They refer to birds which illustrates idea of flying/is relevant to the gist of the passage.

10. Getting the better of gravity (lift acceptable).

11. It involves a creature/animal other than the human participant (gloss of "joining up with another species").

12. The paragraph exemplifies different types of/a variety of birds and their different styles of/competences at flying.

13. Word choice:
    "(persecuted) sorcerers"/"players of the game of quidditch" continues idea of wizards;
    OR
    "Dark Ages" / "sorcerers" and "quidditch" reprise the idea of "throughout history".
    Structure:
    "from … to" construction reprises the idea of "throughout history".

14. Either (Cause) – non-operation/breakdown/ standstill/hold-up (in transport).
    OR (Effect) – (bringing) frustration/boredom.

15. Give the idea of irony/acknowledgement of looseness of meaning/indication that they are not insignificant.

16. Recaps/summarises idea of joy/pleasure/hope/human incapacity to fly.
    OR
    Repeats the idea of looking up given at the outset – ie recognition of cyclical structure of passage.
    OR
    Echoes uplifting tone seen throughout the passage.

English Intermediate 2
Critical Essay 2007

Please see answers to 2008 exam on pages 13-14.

English Intermediate 2
Close Reading 2008

1. There is a contradiction in "hellish yet beautiful"

2. He is not/cannot be sure

3. *Any two from:*
   - similarity in size
   - colour
   - shape
   - contrast with surroundings

4. *Any one from:*
   - The camels drink only twice - we would expect more
   - Walking at night - implies the heat of the day
   - The camels have to carry their own fodder - an additional burden
   - Straw to eat - not nutritious
   - Dry bread/"only…bread, sugar and tea" - unappetising/unvaried//limited range and/or not nutritious

5. *gloss of* "friendly"
   eg welcoming/helpful/hospitable/kindly/nice

   gloss of "flyblown"
   eg rickety/flimsy/ramshackle/makeshift/ uncomfortable/ physically inhospitable/ unhygienic/poor

6. Idea of personification
   eg that it was angry/threatening/bad-tempered

7. "(And) that" refers back to his words in the previous paragraph (about progress/ growth/improvement)

   "was wrong" leads to (the rebuttal contained in) the rest of the paragraph
   OR comment on the linking function of "And"

8. It will happen piecemeal/gradually/without purpose or direction or motive on the part of those who do it.

9. *Glosses of two from:*
   - their produce is pitiful
     eg what they turn out is minimal
   - the climate (is) brutal
     eg the weather is oppressive
   - the distances (are) immense
     eg they have to travel a very long way
   - Salt is already produced as cheaply by industrial means
     eg salt can be obtained equally, efficiently in other ways
   - Market forces [will] kill the trade eg economic factors will overcome them
   - the conscience of the animal rights movement
     eg people concerned with animal welfare will act against them

10. Word choice:
    - "rubbernecking:
      suggests insensitivity/ghoulishness
    - "tourists"
      suggests invasiveness/superficiality
    - "helicopters"
      suggests intrusive modernity
      OR detachment
      OR (financial) contrast

11. - "sprung up"
      suggests an unnatural speed of growth
    - "air-conditioned"
      illustrates the necessity of climate alteration/ modification/control
    - "artificially"
      relates to the idea of falseness
    - "artificially irrigated"
      illustrates the innate dryness/hostility/ uninhabitable quality of the place
    - "bubble"
      suggests its fragility/quality of being insulated from elsewhere

12. Just as seeing something on TV is removed from reality/involvement
    So we are separated from/are removed from/are at a distance from/do not belong to these places

13. Suggests disagreement/cynicism

14. Sad/pessimistic/gloomy/resigned/regretful/ concerned

15. If they are "away from" (pleasant things such as) clean houses/running water/power/schools/adjacent clinic
    Then the expression must mean a harsh/spartan/unpleasant/horrible/ghastly existence

16. (*a*) *Any one from:*
    - Use of parenthesis
    - use of semi-colon
    - repeated use of (clauses starting with) "as"/listing
    - use of (negative) question(s)

    (*b*) *Any two from:*

Feature	Effect
Use of parenthesis	Helps identify/isolate/specify what the "new way of living" is
Semi-colon construction OR use of "as" OR listing	Gives idea of multiplicity and/or variety of ways we are moving away from wilderness
Use of (negative) question(s)	Creates doubt in reader's mind And/or questions wisdom of what we are doing And/or implies agreement with sense of argument

English Intermediate 2
Close Reading 2008 (cont.)

17. Their way of life does not (readily)/conform to (modern) rules and/or boundaries (idea of imposition and/or constriction).
(gloss of "does not fit the pattern of nation states, taxes, frontiers and controls")

18.
- Idea of garden of Eden
  recaps idea of magnificence of place
- Idea of expulsion
  recaps idea of man's desertion of this place
- "of our own accord"
  recaps idea of the leaving being by choice
- "closing the gate behind us"
  recaps idea of irreversibility of process
  OR
  the references to the gates of nature reserves
  OR
  contains an appropriate idea of closure
  OR
  retreating from Nature
- Use of imagery
  matches use of imagery elsewhere (identified)
- Melancholy tone
  matches sombre tone of passage
- The balance of "In the beginning…" and "In the end…"
  is neat
- The balance of "expelled" and "leave it of our own accord"
  is neat

English Intermediate 2
Critical Essay 2008

Please see answers to 2008 exam on pages 13-14.

English Intermediate 2
Critical Essay 2008

Marking principles for Critical Essay are as follows

- Each essay should first be read to establish whether the essay achieves success in **all** the Performance Criteria for Grade C, including relevance and the standards for technical accuracy outlined in Note 1 below.

- If minimum standards are not achieved in any **one** or more of the Performance Criteria, the maximum mark which can be awarded is 11.

- If minimum standards have been achieved, then the supplementary marking grids will allow you to place the work on a scale of marks out of 25.

Notes

1. "Sufficiently accurate" can best be defined in terms of a definition of "consistently accurate".

    - *Consistently accurate*
      A few errors may be present, but these will not be significant in any way. The candidate may use some complex vocabulary and sentence structures. Where appropriate, sentences will show accurate handling of clauses. Linking between sentences will be clear. Paragraphing will reflect a developing line of thought.

    - *Sufficiently accurate*
      As above but with an allowance made for speed and the lack of opportunity to redraft.

2. Using the Category descriptions

    - Categories are not grades. Although derived from performance criteria at C and the indicators of excellence for Grade A, the four categories are designed primarily to assist with placing each candidate response at an appropriate point on a continuum of achievement. Assumptions about final grades or association of final grades with particular categories should not be allowed to influence objective assessment.

    - Once an essay has been deemed to pass the basic criteria, it does not have to meet all the suggestions for Category II (for example) to fall into that Category. More typically there will be a spectrum of strengths and weaknesses which span categories.

Grade C
Performance Criteria

(a) *Understanding*
     As appropriate to task, the response demonstrates understanding of key elements, central concerns and significant details of the text(s).

(b) *Analysis*
     The response explains in some detail ways in which aspects of structure/style/language contribute to meaning/effect/impact.

(c) *Evaluation*
     The response reveals engagement with the text(s) or aspects of the text(s) and stated or implied evaluation of effectiveness, substantiated by some relevant evidence from the text(s).

(d) *Expression*
     Structure, style and language, including use of some appropriate critical terminology, are deployed to communicate meaning clearly and develop a line of thought which is generally relevant to purpose; spelling, grammar and punctuation are sufficiently accurate.

It should be noted that the term "text" encompasses printed, audio or film/video text(s) which may be literary (fiction or non-fiction) or may relate to aspects of media or language.

Language Questions 13-15

- The "text" which should be dealt with in a language question is the research which the pupil has done. Examples taken from their research must be there for you to see.

- However, to demonstrate understanding and analysis related to these examples there has to be some ability to generalise from the particular, to classify and comment on what has been discovered. It is not enough merely to produce a list of words in, say, Dundonian with their standard English equivalents. This is merely description and without any further development does not demonstrate understanding of any principle underlying the choice of words.

- The list of features at the head of the section is supportive. There may be others, but one would expect some of those mentioned would be dealt with.

Intermediate 2 Critical Essay Supplementary Advice

This advice, which is supplementary to the published Performance Criteria, is designed to assist with the placing of scripts within the full range of marks. However, the Performance Criteria as published give the primary definitions. The mark range for each Category is identified.

IV 8–11	III 12–15	II 16–19	I 20–25
• An essay which falls into this category may do so for a variety of reasons. It could be • that it fails to achieve sufficient technical accuracy • or that any knowledge and understanding of the material is not deployed as a response relevant to the task • or that analysis and evaluation attempted are unconvincing • or that the answer is simply too thin.	**Understanding** • Knowledge of the text(s), and a basic understanding of the **main** concerns will be used .... to provide an answer which is **generally relevant** to the task.	**Understanding** • Knowledge and understanding of the **central** concerns of the text(s) will be used .... to provide an answer which is **mainly relevant** to the task.	**Understanding** • **Secure** knowledge **and some insight** into the central concerns of the text(s) will be demonstrated at this level .... and there will be a line of thought **consistently relevant** to the task.
	• Some reference to the text(s) will be made to **support** the candidate's argument.	• Reference to the text(s) will be used as evidence to **promote** the candidate's argument.	• Reference to the text(s) will be used **appropriately** as evidence which helps to **develop** the argument **fully**.
	Analysis • There will be an **explanation** of the contribution of literary/linguistic techniques to the impact of the text(s).	**Analysis** • There will be an **explanation of the effectiveness** of the contribution of literary/linguistic techniques to the impact of the text(s).	**Analysis** • There will be **some insight** shown into the **effectiveness** of the contribution of literary/linguistic techniques to the impact of the text(s).
	Evaluation • There will be **some engagement** with the text(s) which will state or imply an evaluation of its effectiveness.	**Evaluation** • There will be **engagement** with the text(s) which leads to a **generally valid** evaluative stance with respect to the text(s).	**Evaluation** • There will be a **clear engagement** with the text(s) which leads to a **valid** evaluative stance with respect to the material.
	Expression • Language will communicate the argument clearly, and there will be appropriate critical terminology deployed. Spelling, grammar and punctuation will be sufficiently accurate.	**Expression** • Language will communicate the argument **clearly**, and there will be appropriate critical terminology deployed **to aid the argument**. Spelling, grammar and punctuation will be sufficiently accurate.	**Expression** • The language will communicate **effectively** making appropriate use of critical terminology **to further the argument**. Spelling, grammar and punctuation will be sufficiently accurate.

© 2008 Scottish Qualifications Authority/Leckie & Leckie, All Rights Reserved
Published by Leckie & Leckie Ltd, 3rd Floor, 4 Queen Street, Edinburgh EH2 1JE
tel: 0131 220 6831, fax: 0131 225 9987, enquiries@leckieandleckie.co.uk, www.leckieandleckie.co.uk

English Intermediate 2
Close Reading
2004

1. He gives examples of terrifying moments.

   OR

   Reference to an example from the text and appropriate explanation. e.g. "outside a school hall before the start of an exam" conveys clearly a situation of anxiety and fear which is easy to identify with.

2. (a) Reference to the use of either the dash OR the colon introducing the idea that the writer lacks training / knowledge.

   (b) Reference to any one of:
   - "That's right"
   - "dear reader"
   - "your fridge"
   - "I'm"

   (c) Answers should explain that the writer's job is to change a dull reality into something glamorous and provide appropriate reference, e.g. "brown (world) / (of) dry vegetation" becoming "colourful / (and) exciting" **OR** "(nervous," secretive animals" becoming "(an exciting) abundance (of biological complexity)."

3. Answers must explain how "That's" refers to the latter part of the previous paragraph (about the possibility of being attacked), while the whole sentence introduces the writer's real concerns which are the subjects of paragraph 4.

4. The clients will not be told that he is a trainee and he feels desperately lacking in knowledge / information / training

5. Reference to balance / repetition of "One by one" suggesting the names are endless / it's hopeless trying to remember them all / introduction of a humorous tone.

   OR

   Reference to brevity emphasising despair / introducing a humorous tone.

6. It performed as required and enabled him to demonstrate his knowledge.

   OR

   Any reference to being a good example of violence in the bush and / or being something to look at when there's nothing more interesting.

7. His earlier fear that things would go wrong has been realised.

   OR

   His previous lack of confidence has returned.

8. "(I) dutifully (say my piece)"

9. (a) Any two from:

   Sentence structure - short, creating impact of realisation / conveying the thinking process.

   Repetition - "breasted ... breast" / "never, ever" to emphasise how basic his error was
   OR
   "never, ever" to create a childish tone

   Comparison/illustration - blackbird/robin which highlights his mistake

   (b) Any one from:
   - He had run out of things to say.
   - He had found something to talk about.
   - He thought he knew about this bird.

10. Any two from:
    - Not only did he mistake the bird
    - He hadn't noticed / it was one of his clients who'd noticed the giraffes
    - He had scared off the giraffes

11. He refers to a "hurdle (of embarrassment)" suggesting a challenge/series of obstacles.

12. It is a sentence on its own / it is a question which emphasises the unexpectedness of its content / the reader's surprise / that it is an unusual way to end.

13. Answers should deal with:
    - The relevance / effectiveness of "Playing at" (e.g. he was only pretending to be a guide).
    AND
    - The play on words (Guide and Seek / hide and seek).

English Intermediate 2
Critical Essay
2004

Marking principles for Critical Essay are as follows

- Each essay should first be read to establish whether the essay achieves success in all the Performance Criteria for Grade C, including relevance and the standards for technical accuracy outlined in Note 1 below.

- If minimum standards are not achieved in any one or more of the Performance Criteria, the maximum mark which can be awarded is 11.

- If minimum standards have been achieved, then the supplementary marking grids will allow you to place the work on a scale of marks out of 25.

- The Category awarded and the mark should be placed at the end of the essay.

Notes

1. "Sufficiently accurate" can best be defined in terms of a definition of "consistently accurate".

   - *Consistently accurate*
     A few errors may be present, but these will not be significant in any way. The candidate may use some complex vocabulary and sentence structures. Where appropriate, sentences will show accurate handling of clauses. Linking between sentences will be clear. Paragraphing will reflect a developing line of thought.

   - *Sufficiently accurate*
     As above but with an allowance made for speed and the lack of opportunity to redraft.

2. Using the Category descriptions

   - Categories are not grades. Although derived from performance criteria at C and the indicators of excellence for Grade A, the four categories are designed primarily to assist with placing each candidate response at an appropriate point on a continuum of achievement. Assumptions about final grades or association of final grades with particular categories should not be allowed to influence objective assessment.

   - Once an essay has been deemed to pass the basic criteria, it does not have to meet all the suggestions for Category II (for example) to fall into that Category. More typically there will be a spectrum of strengths and weaknesses which span categories.

Grade C
Performance Criteria

(a) *Understanding*
As appropriate to task, the response demonstrates understanding of key elements, central concerns and significant details of the text(s).

(b) *Analysis*
The response explains in some detail ways in which aspects of structure/style/language contribute to meaning/effect/impact.

(c) *Evaluation*
The response reveals engagement with the text(s) or aspects of the text(s) and stated or implied evaluation of effectiveness, substantiated by some relevant evidence from the text(s).

(d) *Expression*
Structure, style and language, including use of some appropriate critical terminology, are deployed to communicate meaning clearly and develop a line of thought which is generally relevant to purpose; spelling, grammar and punctuation are sufficiently accurate.

Intermediate 2 Critical Essay Supplementary Advice

This advice, which is supplementary to the published Performance Criteria, is designed to assist with the placing of scripts within the full range of marks. However, the Performance Criteria as published give the primary definitions. The mark range for each Category is identified.

IV 8–11	III 12–15	II 16–19	I 20–25
• An essay which falls into this category may do so for a variety of reasons. It could be • that it fails to achieve sufficient technical accuracy • or that any knowledge and understanding of the material is not deployed as a response relevant to the task • or that analysis and evaluation attempted are unconvincing • or that the answer is simply too thin.	**Understanding** • Knowledge of the text(s), and a basic understanding of the **main** concerns will be used .... to provide an answer which is **generally relevant** to the task.<hr>• Some reference to the text(s) will be made to **support** the candidate's argument.	**Understanding** • Knowledge and understanding of the **central** concerns of the text(s) will be used .... to provide an answer which is **mainly relevant** to the task.<hr>• Reference to the text(s) will be used as evidence to **promote** the candidate's argument.	**Understanding** • **Secure** knowledge **and some insight** into the central concerns of the text(s) will be demonstrated at this level .... and there will be a line of thought **consistently relevant** to the task.<hr>• Reference to the text(s) will be used **appropriately** as evidence which helps to **develop** the argument **fully**.
	Analysis • There will be an **explanation** of the contribution of literary/linguistic techniques to the impact of the text(s).	**Analysis** • There will be an **explanation of the effectiveness** of the contribution of literary/linguistic techniques to the impact of the text(s).	**Analysis** • There will be **some insight** shown into the **effectiveness** of the contribution of literary/linguistic techniques to the impact of the text(s).
	Evaluation • There will be **some engagement** with the text(s) which will state or imply an evaluation of its effectiveness.	**Evaluation** • There will be **engagement** with the text(s) which leads to a **generally valid** evaluative stance with respect to the text(s).	**Evaluation** • There will be a **clear engagement** with the text(s) which leads to a **valid** evaluative stance with respect to the material.
	Expression • Language will communicate the argument clearly, and there will be appropriate critical terminology deployed. Spelling, grammar and punctuation will be sufficiently accurate.	**Expression** • Language will communicate the argument **clearly**, and there will be appropriate critical terminology deployed **to aid the argument**. Spelling, grammar and punctuation will be sufficiently accurate.	**Expression** • The language will communicate **effectively** making appropriate use of critical terminology **to further the argument**. Spelling, grammar and punctuation will be sufficiently accurate.

English Intermediate 2
Close Reading 2005

1. (a) Any two from:
    - 'gasping for air'
    - 'some interminable mountain slope'
    - 'seems to get steeper at every step'
    - 'trembling'
    - 'disintegrating rock ledge'
    - 'a scrap of cairn'
    - 'some windswept ridge'
    - 'blizzard'
    - 'howls'
    - 'morass'
    - 'sodden peat'
    - ' huddled'

    (b) 'elusive'

2. 'It' is the question 'why am I doing this?'

3. (a) Word Choice: Any one of:
    - 'compulsion' – conveys the strength of his drive to climb
    - 'outlandish' – recognition that it seems mad to go back time after time but he does
    - 'breathless/bruised/battered/bedraggled' – reference to alliteration plus comment **or** comment on the cumulative effect of the words **or** reference to the physical discomfort he may suffer but he is so driven that he still goes back

    (b) Sentence structure: Any one of:
    - Use of (three) questions – (the repeated questioning) shows his struggle to find an answer
    - Use of the list – emphasises the discomforts but he still goes back

4. Any two of:
    - It is a natural instinct ; 'an ancient animal drive'
    - It provides adults with release (of childish fun); 'the Great Outdoors is a giant funhouse' **or** 'we can cast off adult worries and become carefree kids again' 'have no-one give disapproving looks'

5. 'a desire to have fun' refers back to the idea of childish fun as discussed in the previous paragraph and 'there must be more to it' or 'when it ceases to be fun' introduces the idea which he discusses in the rest of the paragraph **or** the sentence is in the form of a question which the rest of the paragraph answers.
A sensible comment on the function of the word 'Yet'.

6. Any three of:
    - Sense of achievement/fulfilment (gloss of 'glow of satisfaction')
    - The fitness achieved (gloss of 'muscles that don't ache/lungs that don't wheeze')
    - Natural exhilaration/pleasure that comes from exercise (gloss of 'endorphins that buzz round your head' or 'keep you feeling high').

7. Any two of:
    - Attitude – critical/sardonic/contemptuous/ doesn't think much of them etc.
      Answers should recognise his negative attitude.
    - Appropriate references to: 'brains have become as useless as their legs'/ – 'banging your head against a brick wall'/'perhaps equating effort with pain'/'laziness'/'do not appear to be able to appreciate'/'such people'

8. That he has retired/he no longer climbs hills/he is dead

9. (a) It introduces answers to the questions posed by the writer

    (b) Questioning/ reflection/ speculation/ pondering/ exploring

10. Any one of:
    - Imagery/Word choice + reference to contrast/balance e.g. Victorian and now or seaside and country or escape and beckons
    - Sentence structure – use of the semi-colon to balance the two parts of the sentence

11. Answers should refer to the Victorian era or to the 1930s and explain i.e. gloss on 'dark satanic mills' or 'depressed thirties'

12. Answers should include:
    - Understanding of image in relation to content
    - intensity of personal need
    - relationship to the initial question in the title – Why?
    - brevity effective as a conclusion

[BLANK PAGE]

[BLANK PAGE]

[BLANK PAGE]

Acknowledgements

Leckie & Leckie is grateful to the copyright holders, as credited, for permission to use their material.
The Sunday Times for the article 'Playing at Guide and Seek' by Sean Newsom, 2001 © NI Syndication, London (2004 Close Reading pp 2-3); Luath Press for an extract from *The Joy of Hillwalking* by Ralph Storer (2005 Close Reading pp 2-3).
The Times for an article by Matthew Parris, 25th February 2006 (2008 Close Reading pp 2-3)

The following companies have very generously given permission to reproduce their copyright material free of charge:
Glenda Cooper for the article 'Women and chocolate: Simply made for each other' (2006 Close Reading pp 2-3)
Short Books for an extract from *How to Be a Bad Birdwatcher* by Simon Barnes (2007 Close Reading pp 2-3)